Comptroller of the Currency
Administrator of National Banks

# Capital Accounts and Dividends

Comptroller's Handbook
(Section 303)

Narrative - August 1991,  Procedures - March 1998

Capital

# Capital Accounts and Dividends (Section 303)

# Table of Contents

# Capital Accounts and Dividends (Section 303)    Introduction

Determining the adequacy of a bank's capital is important, not only to assess the strength of an individual bank, but also to evaluate the safety and soundness of the entire banking system. The OCC is also required to analyze capital adequacy in taking action on various types of applications such as mergers and branches. Bank capital helps to:

- Assure public confidence in the stability of individual banks and the commercial banking system.

- Support the volume, type, and character of the business conducted.

- Provide for the possibilities of inherent loss.

- Assure the risks in commercial banking are distributed appropriately between the private and banking sector.

- Permit the bank to continue to meet the reasonable credit requirements of their delineated community.

Therefore, the supervisory process must continually assess whether a bank's level of capital is sufficient to permit it to operate as a viable institution. A comprehensive evaluation of capital adequacy considers a wide range of both quantitative and qualitative factors. Quantitative measures of capital adequacy are commonly expressed as ratios. Qualitative factors include, among other things, a bank's liquidity position, management quality, asset quality, and earnings capacity.

## Quantitative Factors

## Evolution of Capital Adequacy Measures

Federal banking agencies have historically employed minimum supervisory ratios relating capital to total assets in the assessment of capital adequacy of banks. These ratios have evolved over time. Definitional and technical changes have been made in the methods used to calculate minimum capital ratios.

In 1985, as mandated by the International Lending Supervision Act of 1983, the OCC, along with the other Federal banking agencies, adopted similar regulations intended to foster further improvement in bank capital ratios and eliminate the disparities in treatment of federally regulated banks with respect to capital adequacy. The OCC's minimum capital regulation codified as 12 CFR 3, defined capital, set required minimum capital ratios, established procedures for setting higher minimums and issuing capital directives. At that time, the OCC also proposed to study various methods of deriving a risk-asset based ratio.

Under the auspices of the Bank for International Settlements' Committee on Banking Regulations and Supervisory Practices (the Basle Committee), Federal banking regulators worked with the supervisory authorities of eleven other member nations to develop a common framework for measuring capital adequacy, including minimum capital standards for internationally active banks. The international agreement was formally approved in July, 1988 and has been adopted by 25 countries (Australia, Austria, Belgium, Canada, Denmark, Finland, France, Germany, Greece, Iceland, Ireland, Italy, Japan, Luxembourg, Netherlands, New Zealand, Norway, Portugal, Saudi Arabia, Spain, Sweden, Switzerland, Turkey, United Kingdom, and United States).

## Risk-Based Capital Guidelines

Based on the international framework, the OCC, in conjunction with the Federal Deposit Insurance Corporation (FDIC) and the Board of Governors of the Federal Reserve System, developed and adopted final risk-based capital guidelines for all U.S. banks. The guidelines also apply to bank holding companies with consolidated assets of $150 million or more.

The risk-based capital guidelines represent a significant step in the measurement of capital adequacy for several reasons. First, the guidelines strengthen the quality of capital by increasing the emphasis on common equity and by restricting the amount of loan loss reserves that can be counted as capital. Second, the guidelines recognize the relative degree of credit risk associated with various assets by setting different capital requirements for some assets that clearly have less credit risk than others. Third, banks are required to hold capital against their off-balance sheet activities in a systematic manner. Fourth, the guidelines will aid in making the definition of capital and the minimum standards uniform internationally.

The risk-based capital requirement becomes effective on December 31, 1990. Until that date, the requirements for primary and total capital contained in the existing regulation (12 CFR Part 3) will continue to be operative. However, banks are expected to begin working with the new guidelines prior to December 31, 1990, taking whatever steps are necessary to ensure that they will be able to comply with these guidelines when they become effective.

The risk-based capital guidelines provide for a two-year transition period beginning on December 31, 1990, during which certain requirements within the guidelines are relaxed, and the minimum risk-based capital ratio will be 7.25 percent. On December 31, 1992, the guidelines will take effect in their final form, and all banks will be required to have and maintain a minimum risk-based capital ratio of 8 percent.

It should be emphasized that the risk-based capital guidelines establish a minimum capital ratio, and that most banks, as is the case presently, will be expected to maintain a capital ratio that is above the minimum. The primary focus of the risk- based capital guidelines is credit risk. The guidelines do not explicitly address other types of risk that can affect a bank's condition, such as asset quality, interest-rate risk, asset concentrations, and operational risk. Therefore, the level of capital required for an individual bank will depend on that institution's total risk profile, as determined through the supervisory process.

## Risk-Based Capital Ratio

A bank's risk-based capital ratio is calculated by dividing the capital base (numerator) by risk-weighted assets (denominator). Risk-weighted assets include balance sheet assets and off- balance-sheet items in proportion to their relative credit risk.

Balance sheet assets are assigned to one of four risk categories—0 percent, 20 percent, 50 percent, and 100 percent—based on their relative riskiness. The risk weight is determined by looking at the obligor and, in some cases, the guarantor or the collateral. For example, U.S. government securities are in the 0 percent risk category and, therefore, are not included in the risk-weighted assets total. At the opposite end of the spectrum, the typical commercial or installment loan (other than a residential mortgage loan) is in the 100 percent risk category requiring a full measure of capital. A full summary of risk-weights and categories is detailed in 12 CFR Part 3, Appendix A, Table 1.

Off-balance sheet items are captured in two steps. First, a credit equivalent is calculated for the off-balance sheet instrument using one of the four credit conversion factors—0, 20, 50, or 100 percent. The appropriate conversion factor is determined by the type of activity. This first step produces a figure that is roughly comparable to the face value of balance sheet assets. The second step assigns the credit equivalent to one of the four risk categories using the same criteria as balance sheet assets—obligor, guarantor, or collateral—to come up with a risk-weighted value like that for balance sheet assets. A schedule of credit conversion factors for off- balance-sheet items is contained in 12 CFR Part 3, Appendix A, Table 2.

## Collateral and Guarantees

Only certain types of collateral held by the bank reduce the risk-weighting of the related asset. For example, cash on deposit in the bank, securities issued by or guaranteed by the U.S. government or its agencies, and securities issued by or guaranteed by U.S. government-sponsored agencies can reduce the risk-weighting of an asset to 20 percent. Similarly, only certain types of guarantees qualify an asset for a lower risk weight. Risk-weightings are reduced only for the portions of assets covered by such guarantees or the current market value of recognized collateral.

One important distinction is made with regard to the guarantees of central governments, including the U.S. government and its agencies. To receive a 0 percent risk weight, the guarantee must be unconditional. A conditional guarantee requires certain affirmative actions, usually servicing standards, to maintain the validity of the guarantee. Most guarantees offered by the U.S. government and its agencies are conditional and, therefore, place the asset in the 20 percent category, rather than 0 percent. This distinction only applies to central government guarantees that would otherwise merit a 0 percent risk-weight and, therefore, require no capital to be held against those assets.

# Definition of Capital

Under the guidelines, capital is divided into two tiers. Core Capital (Tier 1) is defined as the sum of core capital components, less goodwill and other non-qualifying intangibles. Tier 1 includes the purest and most stable forms of capital—common shareholder's equity (common stock, surplus, and retained earnings), noncumulative perpetual preferred stock, and minority interests in the equity accounts of consolidated subsidiaries.

Supplementary (Tier 2) capital includes all cumulative perpetual and limited-life preferred stock, hybrid capital instruments, including mandatory convertible securities, term debt, and the allowance for loan and lease losses (ALLL), subject to certain limitations.

Under the guidelines, Tier 2 capital in excess of 100 percent of Tier 1 capital may not be applied to meet the regulatory minimums. This fundamental feature emphasizes Tier 1 capital in the adequacy determination. There are other limits applied to certain Tier 2 elements; for example, the ALLL can be included as capital only up to 1.25 percent of total risk-weighted assets. This limitation ensures that most of a bank's reserves that are already earmarked to cover likely losses are excluded from capital. Further, to guard against over-reliance on nonperpetual capital, the sum of term debt and intermediate- term preferred stock may be included only up to a total of 50 percent of Tier 1 capital. Moreover, limited-life capital instruments must be amortized over the last five years of their term.

# Deductions from Capital

In calculating a risk-based capital ratio, certain items are deducted from the appropriate portion of a bank's capital base to derive the numerator. Goodwill is generally deducted from Tier 1 capital, except as permitted by the transition rules.

Most other identifiable intangible assets are also deducted from Tier 1 capital unless they satisfy guideline criteria relating to severability, marketability, and demonstrable market values based on identifiable cash flows. Identifiable intangibles, such as purchased mortgage servicing rights, that satisfy the criteria may remain in the bank's Tier 1 capital provided in the aggregate they do not exceed 25 percent of Tier 1 capital.

In addition, investments in unconsolidated banking and finance subsidiaries and international reciprocal holdings of capital instruments of other banking organizations are deducted from total capital. A complete schedule of capital components is contained in 12 CFR Part 3, Appendix A, Table 4.

## Transition Provisions

The risk-based capital guidelines will be phased in over time with full implementation on December 31, 1992. The final risk-based capital guidelines require banks to hold a minimum total risk-based capital ratio of 8 percent as of December 31, 1992. Of this 8 percent, at least half must be composed of Tier 1 capital. However, a transition period is provided, beginning on December 31, 1990 and ending on December 30, 1992. During that period, banks will be required to meet an interim minimum total risk-based capital ratio of 7.25 percent, using certain transitional rules that are detailed in section 4 of the risk-based capital guidelines.

Banks should immediately begin monitoring their risk-based capital ratios and working toward achieving the interim and final minimum ratios. Any bank that has risk-based capital ratios of less than 4 percent Tier 1 capital and 8 percent total capital should be developing a plan to achieve those standards by December 31, 1992 as well as the interim ratio of 7.25 percent by December 31, 1990. Furthermore, banks that at present have risk-based capital in excess of the 8 percent minimum should not take any action that would cause their risk-based capital ratio to fall below 8 percent.

The 8 percent risk-based capital ratio is a minimum, and most banks will be expected to maintain risk-based capital levels that exceed the 8 percent minimum. This ratio is considered a minimum because, although the risk-based capital standard focuses primarily on credit risk, a bank's capital base must also be available to absorb losses stemming from other types of risk. Therefore, the OCC will continue to assess both the quality of risk management systems and the level of overall risk in individual banks through the supervisory process and will require additional capital when warranted. In addition, work will continue within the Basle Committee on developing a common international approach to assessing interest rate risk and exchange rate risk.

An assessment of overall capital adequacy takes into account these and other risks and involves a qualitative judgment made in conjunction with the OCC's supervision of national banks. This assessment involves analysis of the quality and level of earnings, the quality of loans and investments, the effectiveness of loan and investment policies, and management's overall ability to monitor and control risk. Thus, the assessment of a banking organization's capital adequacy goes far beyond a simple risk-based capital ratio. Nevertheless, the risk-based ratio provides bankers and examiners an important benchmark or starting point for analysis of capital adequacy.

## Minimum Leverage Ratio

The OCC intends to amend its existing capital regulation, 12 CFR Part 3. When adopted, these amendments would supplement the risk-based capital guidelines with a minimum leverage ratio, using the new definition of capital as a percentage of total assets. Therefore, a national bank is expected to maintain capital to satisfy both the risk-based capital requirement and the minimum leverage ratio.

The OCC believes that a minimum leverage ratio is necessary because the risk-based capital guidelines, which are designed solely as a measure of credit risk, create the possibility for significant leverage. Assets that have no credit risk receive a 0 percent risk weight and, therefore, require no capital. However, the OCC believes that every bank should have at least a base level of capital as protection against the other banking risks such as interest rate, liquidity, operational, and concentration risks that are not measured by the risk-based capital ratio. A minimum leverage ratio based on total assets would establish such a base level of capital for all banks.

## Qualitative Factors

Although both the risk-based capital ratio and the minimum leverage ratio are important quantitative tools in measuring and regulating capital adequacy, there are numerous qualitative risk factors that must be considered. The OCC has traditionally recognized that banks are exposed to varying degrees and types of risk, and, therefore, any comprehensive capital-adequacy determination must be made on a case-by-case basis.

Some of the more important qualitative factors affecting capital are explained

---

below. Supervisory evaluations of capital adequacy should take into account the influence these factors may have on a particular bank:

- Quality of Management—The quality, experience, depth, and sophistication of bank management is perhaps most significant in determining capital adequacy. Sound management entails implementing and monitoring policies and procedures, internal controls, and audit coverage. The absence of strong supervision, because of inept or dishonest management, will ultimately lead to a deterioration of bank capital.

- Funds Management—Funds management is the core of sound bank planning and financial management. It includes the supervision of bank liquidity and interest rate sensitivity. Each bank should have procedures to minimize the possibility of liquidity risk that could result in forced asset sales or interest rate risk that could result from asset maturities that are mismatched with source fund maturities.

- Earnings and Their Retention—A bank's current and historical earnings is another key element in assessing capital adequacy. Good earnings' performance enables a bank to expand, remain competitive, and augment its capital funds. The bank's dividend policy is also of importance. Excessive dividends can weaken a bank's capital position. A history of low dividend payments may impede efforts to issue new equity. Banks located in rapidly growing markets must be attentive to their rate of earnings' retention so they may properly plan for new capital funds as needed.

- Asset Quality—The risk-weighting of assets under the Risk-Based Capital Guidelines accounts for the relative credit risk of different instruments. However, the guidelines cannot account for weak or valueless assets held by a financial institution. Lower quality assets have a greater potential for loss and should be reflected in a stronger capital base.

- Risk Diversification—Generally, a greater degree of defined asset and liability concentrations increases the need for capital in most banks. On- and off-balance sheet assets should be reviewed for concentrations in industries, product lines customer types, funding sources, and nonbank activities.

- Ownership—The objectives and financial status of a bank's ownership are important considerations since they can significantly affect the condition and direction of a bank. This influence usually is more pronounced when ownership is concentrated. Typically, financially distressed or self-serving ownership will erode capital adequacy over a period of time. Conversely, a very conservative philosophy may be detrimental in the face of progressive competition.

- Operating Procedures and Controls—Inefficient or lax operations are costly to a bank. Shortcomings in systems, procedures, and controls expose a bank to loss through fraud, defalcation, or employee error.

- Strategic Planning—A dynamic planning process is essential in light of the intense competition within the financial services industry. Banks that identify potential changes in their environment or operations may soon find their financial viability in question.

Banks subject to greater risks include newly chartered institutions, banks receiving special supervisory attention, those experiencing rapid growth, or banks that may be affected through activities of its holding company and affiliates.

## Capital Accounts

In addition to determining the adequacy of capital, the examination of capital accounts entails a review and analysis of changes which have occurred or are contemplated, including those in ownership of bank stock. Accounts the examiner reviewing capital will examine are those included in the OCC's definition of capital except for the allowance for loan and lease losses and subordinated notes and debentures.

Records detailing the number of shares authorized, issued, unissued, and the par value for each class of stock should be maintained in the working papers. Changes in these items should be investigated to determine that necessary approvals have been obtained and that the articles of association have been amended, as required.

Various statutory limitations imposed on banks are determined by the amount of the capital accounts. Testing for compliance with those limitations may necessitate calculating many limits. The examiner performing this program computes all capital-based limits applicable to a bank and distributes the results to appropriate examining personnel.

The examiner must be concerned with the ownership of the bank because shareholders directly influence its course through their election of directors. When a bank is owned or controlled by one person or a small group, the impact is obvious. With cumulative voting of stock, however, a shareholder who owns less than a controlling interest may still be able to elect one or more directors and thus significantly affect the direction of the bank. Generally, the identity of any shareholder or group who owns or controls five percent or more of any class of stock should become a part of the examiner's records. The method by which changes in ownership occur should be reviewed and analyzed for all banks. In banks that have actively traded stock, market acceptance of that stock may be a good indicator of the financial community's attitude toward the institution. In a smaller bank that has a predominantly local market for its stock, information on local residents' interest in purchasing the bank's stock can prove to be beneficial.

Many small banks do not have an established market for their stock. In such cases, an officer or director may find a buyer for the stock of shareholders who wish to sell. A person who provides that service must avoid using insider information in any transaction. One way to eliminate the possibility of a conflict of interest or the use of insider information is for the bank to maintain a list of people interested in purchasing stock. Any prospective seller can then examine the list and sell to an interested buyer at a mutually agreed upon price.

Legislative amendments in 1978 gave the OCC some regulatory authority over the quality and character of ownership. Any person who proposes directly or indirectly to acquire control of 25 percent or more of a national bank's voting stock is required to give the OCC 60 days prior notice. The notice is filed with the Deputy Comptroller (District) either on Form CC 7028-36, Notice of Change in Control of a National Bank, or in any other format that provides all of the information required by 12 USC 1817(j)(6). The OCC may disapprove the proposed change in control for reasons contained in 12 USC 1817(j)(7). Certain types of transactions listed in 12 CFR 5.50 are exempt from the notice requirement.

# Dividends

Dividends are distributions of earnings to owners. For a dividend to be declared, the board of directors must take formal action to designate the medium of payment, the dividend rate, the shareholder record date and date of payment. The bank must record dividends as a liability when they are declared.

Although dividends are usually declared and paid in either cash or stock, occasionally they are used to distribute real or personal property. This latter transaction is a "dividend-in-kind." Information on procedures for obtaining OCC approval for changes in equity capital, including dividends-in-kind, can be found in the Comptroller's Manual for Corporate Activities.

Stock dividends are distributions of additional shares to stockholders in proportion to the number of shares they own They must be reported by transferring an amount equal to the fair value of the additional shares from undivided profits to a category of permanent capitalization (common stock and surplus). The amount transferred from undivided profits may not be less than the par or stated value of the additional shares. All stock dividends are subject to 12 CFR 5.46. The OCC believes recurring stock dividends should relate to earnings. Those dividends also must comply with the requirements of 12 USC 56 and 60.

All dividends must conform to applicable statutory requirements. Under 12 USC 56, a national bank may not pay a dividend on its common stock if the dividend would exceed net undivided profits then on hand. Further, under 12 USC 60, a national bank must obtain prior approval from the OCC to pay dividends on either common or preferred stock that would exceed its net profits for the current year combined with retained net profits (net profits minus dividends paid during that period) of the prior two years. In an enforcement action, the OCC may require a hank to seek prior approval from the OCC for any proposed dividends.

## Prior Approval

Any enforcement action that requires a notional bank to raise additional capital or to maintain a certain level of capital also should require the hank to obtain prior approval from the OCC before paying a dividend. In cases where prior approval is not required, examiners should consider requiring prior notice to the OCC before a dividend is paid. In developing an enforcement action that includes capital considerations, the supervisory office should document in SMS the justification for not requiring prior approval of dividends.

A requirement to seek prior approval for a dividend does not prohibit a bank from paying dividends. Rather, it provides the OCC an opportunity to review the bank's status and future prospects to determine whether payment of the proposed dividend would result in an unsafe or unsound condition detrimental to the best interests of the bank. Procedures for reviewing requests for prior approval may be found in Examining Circular 257.

## Permissible Dividends

In January 1, 1991, the OCC made some changes to interpretations of the dividend regulations to simplify the calculation of a bank's dividend paying capacity and make them more consistent with generally accepted accounting principles (GAAP). Under the old interpretations, some banks mistakenly believed they could add back their allowance for loan and lease losses (ALLL) to undivided profits to compute the available capital for 12 USC 56. That was not the OCC's policy.

The OCC's clarification specifically prohibits the addition of the ALLL to undivided profits then on hand for applying the 12 USC 56 test. However, the rule allows bad debts, which must be deducted from undivided profits, to be offset against the ALLL, so that only the excess is deducted. Statutory bad debts are obligations that are past due more than six months and that are not both well secured and in the process of collection.

Banks had commonly interpreted net profits available to pay dividends in 12 USC 60 as equalling net income plus the provision for loan losses less net loan charge-offs. Under the new interpretation, "net profits" for dividend purposes equals net income as reported in the bank's call report with no adjustments.

The dividend limit in 12 USC 60 is based on retained net profits for the current plus the two previous years. The net profits definition change was effective for all banks beginning January 1, 1991. However, a phase-in option is available. In calculating 1991 net profits, a bank may elect to apply the new definition retroactively for all years from 1989. Alternately, a bank may use the new definition for net profits for 1991 and subsequent years, while relying on the old definition for 1989 and 1990 net profits. Once a bank elects to recompute the net profits for 1989 or 1990 using the new definition, it must use that approach for every year thereafter.

## Unsafe and Unsound Dividends

There are situations in which a national bank should not pay a dividend even if that dividend would be in compliance with the provisions of 12 USC 56 and 60. For example, paying dividends that deplete a bank's capital base to an inadequate level constitutes an unsafe and unsound banking practice. Complying with the regulations governing minimum capital requirements and payment of cash dividends does not relieve directors of their fiduciary responsibility to operate the bank in a safe and sound manner. The board of directors should ensure that any proposed dividend Is consistent with the bank's projections, capital plan and strategic plan, and will not have an adverse impact on the bank's long-term capital adequacy. Even if a proposed dividend would not reduce capital below the required level, the directors may decide not to issue a dividend because they wish to preserve capital that is strained by increasing levels of problem assets, plans for significant growth, or other inherent risks.

Examiners should review all dividends to ensure they are consistent with projections, capital plan and strategic plan, and they would not have an adverse impact on long-term capital adequacy.

## Transfer Agent Activities

Many national banks act as transfer agents for their own securities, for securities of parent holding companies, as for securities of other corporations. The provisions of 12 USC 92(a) limit banks without trust powers to performing transfer agent functions solely for their own securities or for securities of affiliates.

A transfer agent maintains and updates the master securityholder file, which is the official list of individual securityholder accounts. The transfer agent must record promptly and accurately all changes in ownership of securities to the master securityholder file.

The master securityholder file should contain, at a minimum, the following detail:

- The certificate number.
- The number of shares for equity securities or the principal dollar amount for debt securities.
- The securityholder's registration.
- The address of the registered securityholder.
- The issue date of the security.
- The cancellation date of the security.

The cancellation date is added to the certificate detail in the master securityholder file when a certificate is presented for transfer and is canceled by the transfer agent. The transfer agent then prepares a new certificate(s) for the new owner and adds the new certificate detail listed above to the master securityholder file.

Preventing the overissuance of a security is the responsibility of a registrar, who maintains a record or document that shows the total number of shares or the principal dollar amount authorized and issued by the issuer. Ordinarily, a transfer agent will also perform the registrar function. The term "registrar" is also used to refer to transfer agents of debt securities.

Examiners must be alert for instances when the bank is acting as transfer agent for its own securities or for securities of an affiliate which are registered under Section 12 of the Securities Exchange Act of 1934. Transfer agents that perform transfer agent functions for registered securities must adhere to a number of regulatory requirements of the Securities and Exchange Commission (SEC). The SEC regulations were established to assure that all securities transfers are conducted in a prompt and accurate manner and to establish an early warning system for inadequate transfer agent performance.

Any national bank performing transfer agent functions for its own or any other securities registered under Section 12 of the Securities Exchange Act of 1934 must register as a transfer agent by filing Form TA-1 with the Office of the Comptroller of the Currency (OCC). The registration of a transfer agent becomes effective 30 days after receipt of Form TA-1 by the OCC, unless the filing does not comply with applicable requirements, or the OCC takes affirmative action to accelerate, deny, or postpone registration. Each registrant must amend Form TA-1 within 60 calendar days following the date on which information reported in it becomes inaccurate, incomplete, or misleading.

A registered transfer agent must adhere to regulations issued by the SEC. The significant provisions include:

- 17 CFR 240.17f-2, Fingerprinting of Transfer Agent Personnel—This rule requires that anyone who is directly involved in handling certificates, securityholder records, or related monies and persons with regular access thereto must be fingerprinted and have their fingerprints forwarded to the FBI for identification. Bank directors, officers, and employees can be exempt from fingerprinting if they meet the following conditions:

  - Not engage in the sale of securities.
  - Not have regular access to the processing of securities, original transfer agent records, or monies related to transfer agent activities.
  - Not have direct supervision over persons engaged in those activities.

- 17 CFR 240.17Ad-2, Turnaround of Items—This rule requires registered transfer agents to turnaround, within three business days of receipt, at least 90 percent of all routine items received for transfer during a month. The term "item" means a certificate or certificates of a single issue of securities presented for transfer by one presenter at one time. An item is routine unless it is:

  - Accompanied by a special instruction or supporting documentation that requires review before transfer can be effected.
  - Subjected to a restriction on transfer.
  - Presented in connection with a corporate reorganization, tender offer, etc.
  - Of an issue that was offered to the public within the previous 15 business days. National banks can be exempt from this rule if they have received fewer than 500 items for transfer during the most recent 6-month period.

- 17 CFR 240.17Ad-4, Exempt Transfer Agents—This rule provides that registered transfer agents are exempt from the three- business-day-turnaround rule and certain parts of other regulations if they have received fewer than 500 items for transfer during the latest 6-month period. To obtain exempt status, the transfer agent must prepare and maintain in its possession a document certifying that it qualifies as exempt. The exemption remains in effect as long as the 500-item threshold is not exceeded.

- 17 CFR 240.17Ad-11, Reports of Record Differences—A "record difference" occurs when either: (1) the number of shares or principal dollar amount in the master securityholder file does not equal the number of shares or principal dollar amount authorized and issued; or (2) a security transferred or redeemed contains certificate detail (registration, amount, maturity date, etc.) different from the certificate detail currently on the master securityholder file, which difference cannot be immediately resolved. This rule sets forth conditions under which transfer agents must report record differences to issuers and to the OCC. In cases where an actual physical overissuance has occurred, transfer agents have to resolve the record difference within six months; otherwise, they are required to purchase in the open market ("buy in") an amount of securities sufficient to reduce the record differences (17 CFR 240.17Ad-10).

## General Procedures

To avoid duplication of effort, some steps in these procedures require the examiner to gather or review information obtained from examiners reviewing other areas of the bank's operations.  The examiner should obtain information not available from other examiners directly from the bank.  As appropriate, the examiner should cross-reference working papers with other examination sections.

Objective: To determine the scope of the examination of capital and dividends.

1.    Review the following documents to identify areas that require follow-up. Examples include:

☐ Previous capital and dividends examination findings and bank management's response to those findings.
☐ Memorandum from the examiner assigned Internal and External Audit.  If internal/external audit is not part of the overall scope of the current examination, review the work performed in this area by the bank's internal/external auditors.  Obtain a list of any deficiencies noted in the latest internal/external auditor report and determine if the bank has taken appropriate corrective action.
☐ Supervisory Strategy and Scope Memorandum issued by the Examiner-In-Charge.
☐ Information on capital directives, if applicable.
☐ Internal bank reports on capital and dividends including risk-based capital.  Examples include:
   – Budget(s).
   – Strategic plan.
   – Excerpts from board minutes and board reports.

2.    Obtain appropriate schedules from the Call Report and run capital model to approximate the bank's risk-based capital.

3.    Calculate the following limits (QCALC may be used as a tool) and

distribute them to the examiners assigned the appropriate areas:

- Investment in securities (12 U.S.C. 24).
- Establishment of branches (12 U.S.C. 36(c)).
- Extension of credit (12 U.S.C. 84).
- Aggregate extensions of credit to executive officers, directors, and principal shareholders and their related interests (12 U.S.C. 375b(5)(A) and 12 CFR 215.4(d)(1)).
- Extension of loans to affiliates (12 U.S.C. 371c).
- Investment in bank premises (12 U.S.C. 371d).
- Deposits maintained with depository institutions that do not have access to Federal Reserve advances (12 U.S.C. 463).

4.    Update shareholder information for working papers and applicable OCC databases.  Consider:

- Full and correct list of the names and residences of all shareholders and the number of shares held by each is maintained, and that such a list is available to all shareholders and creditors of the bank (12 U.S.C. 62).

- Information regarding the stock holdings of directors, their families, and beneficial interests.  Prepare a list of major shareholders which includes the percent of ownership of the bank they control and their related interests with the bank.

- For a bank acting as its own transfer agent and/or registrar, a list of transactions engaged in since the last examination.  Include the following information about the transactions:
    - New shareholder's name.
    - Number of shares.
    - Certificate number offsetting with prior shareholder's name(s).
    - Number of shares surrendered.
    - Certificate number(s).

Based on the performance of the preceding steps and discussions with the bank EIC and other appropriate OCC supervisors, determine the scope and set the objectives of this examination.

# Quantity of Risk

**Conclusion:** The quantity of risk is (low, moderate, high).

**Objective:** To determine whether the level of capital and dividends is appropriate.

1. Review any material changes or unusual items and fluctuations in the bank's capital and dividend accounts since the previous examination. Consider:

   - Preferred stock, including limited life preferred stock.
   - Common stock.
   - Surplus.
   - Undivided profits.
   - Valuation reserves for securities.
   - Reserves for contingencies.
   - Other accounts representing segregation of undivided profits.
   - Mandatory convertible instruments.

2. Review UBPR, BERT, QCALC, and other OCC database reports for positive and adverse trends that may affect capital levels.

3. Determine whether the bank's capital and dividends position is compatible with the complexity, size, and risk profile of the institution's assets and operations.

**Objective:** To determine the effect of credit quality on capital.

1. Evaluate through discussions with examiner assigned Loan Portfolio Management to what extent credit quality adversely affects the adequacy of capital. Consider:

   - Level and trends of classified, special mention, and nonperforming assets.

   - The impact of current and potential loan and lease losses as well as applicable qualitative factors contained in the bank's analysis of the ALLL.

   - Input from other examination areas, such as Investment Securities.

   - Impact of other assets, contingent accounts, or off-balance sheet accounts.

**Objective:** To determine the effects of other risks on capital.

1. Determine to what extent other risks affect capital adequacy. Consider:

- Whether the bank's analysis/planning process considers any additional capital charge for non-credit risks (e.g., interest rate risk, liquidity risk, price risk, foreign exchange risk, transaction risk, or reputation risk).

- If shortcomings in internal controls, audit procedures, or compliance processes could weaken the bank's capital base by making it more susceptible to substantive violations or loss through fraud or defalcation.

- That capital is sufficient to compensate for any noted instabilities or deficiencies in the quality and structure of the bank's assets and liabilities (for example large amounts of asset depreciation within the balance sheet).

- Whether the bank's present and projected deposit and borrowed funds structure is supported by present and projected capital.

- That capital is sufficient to compensate for the volume of off- balance sheet assets and support nontraditional activities.

Objective: To determine the effect of strategic decisions on capital.

1. Evaluate the bank's strategic or capital plan. Consider:

   - Whether the bank's capital structure is considered in the strategic planning process.

   - Whether growth assumptions are reasonable.

   - Whether present and projected dividends are considered excessive. If excessive, analyze the resulting impact on capital, particularly if such dividends were or are to be paid to encourage the success of an equity offering.

   - Whether plans for new product lines and other measures to remain competitive are supported by present and projected capital.

2. Determine if the quality and strength of earnings enable the bank to:

   - Fund its expansion adequately.
   - Replenish or increase its capital funds as needed.

3. Determine if management is considering a public or private offering of bank stock or subordinated notes or debentures. Consider:

- The impact on capital levels.
- Potential changes in control or the dilution of shareholder interests, if any.
- The potential purchaser's aspirations regarding control.
- The cost of increasing shareholders' equity versus debt equity obligations.
- The net effect convertible instruments will have on capital.
- The level of underwriting expenses.

4. Determine if any change has occurred in preferred stock, common stock, authorized but unissued stock, or subordinated debentures that relate to a specific strategic initiative. Consider:

- Notifying the examiner assigned to review "Duties and Responsibilities of Directors."

- Determining that any conversion of preferred stock or debt instrument complied with the terms of the agreement.

- Determining that management has complied with the requirements of 12 CFR Part 5.

## Objective: To determine the market's perception of the bank's value.

1. Obtain reports of bank stock pledged elsewhere and determine that directors own qualifying shares (See 12 USC 72 and 12 CFR 7.2005).

2. If the bank's stock is listed, prepare/update and analyze historical trends of the bank's stock market prices. Consider:

- Listing highs and lows on a quarterly and end-of-period basis.
- Contains quotes with related price/earning ratios over the last several years.

3. If the bank's stock is unlisted and the chief executive officer or board members maintain market information for the stock, consider:

- Who quotes the price and how the price is determined.

- If any favorable sales and purchases involve insiders (by reviewing transactions).

- Whether the bank maintains a list of individuals who have expressed an interest in the stock, and, if so, ensure that the list of prospective purchasers is available to any shareholder interested in selling stock.

- Whether stock is selling at a reasonable multiple of earnings.

Objective: Determine the level of compliance with regulatory requirements.

1. Evaluate compliance with 12 CFR Part 3.

For Total Capital, determine the following requirements:

- A minimum ratio of total capital (after deductions) to risk-weighted assets of 8 percent (12 CFR 3.6(a); 12 CFR Part 3, Appendix A, Section 4(b)(1), and Table 4).

- Deductions from total capital that reflect:

    - Equity and debt investments in unconsolidated banking and finance subsidiaries that are deemed to be capital of the subsidiary (12 CFR 3, Section 2(c)(3)(I)).

    - Reciprocal holdings of bank capital instruments (12 CFR 3, Section 2(c)(3)(ii)).

For Tier 1 Capital requirements determine:

- For a bank with a CAMEL composite rating of 1, that Tier 1 capital is equal to at least 3 percent of adjusted total assets (12 CFR 3.6(b); 12 CFR Part 3, Appendix A, Section 4(b)(3).

- For a bank with a CAMEL composite rating other than 1, that Tier 1 capital is equal to at least 3 percent of adjusted total assets plus an additional cushion of at least 100 to 200 basis points or 4 to 5 percent leverage ratio (12 CFR 3.6(c); 12 CFR Part 3, Appendix A, Section 4(b)(3).
**Note: Change in regulation pending.**

- That Tier 1 capital reflects:

    - Only common stockholder's equity, noncumulative perpetual preferred stock and related surplus, and minority interests in the equity accounts of consolidated subsidiaries (12 CFR Part 3, Appendix A, Section 2(a)).

    - A deduction of goodwill (12 CFR Part 3, Appendix A, Section 2(c)(1)(I)).

    - A deduction of disallowed intangible assets (12 CFR Part 3, Appendix A, Section 2(c)(1)(ii)).

- A deduction of deferred tax assets (12 CFR Part 3, Appendix A, Section 2(c)(1)(iii)).

- Any intangible assets included as Tier 1 capital are limited to mortgage servicing assets and purchased credit card relationships (12 CFR Part 3, Appendix A, Section 2(c)(2)). In addition:

  - The total of all intangible assets included in Tier 1 capital is limited to 50 percent of Tier 1 capital (12 CFR Part 3, Appendix A, Section 2(c)(2)(I)). **Note: Change in regulation pending.**

  - No more than 25 percent of Tier 1 capital consists of purchased credit card relationships (12 CFR Part 3, Appendix A, Section 2(c)(2)(I)).

  - Calculation of these limitations is based on Tier 1 capital net of goodwill and other disallowed intangible assets.

  - Each intangible asset included in Tier 1 capital is valued in accordance with 12 CFR Part 3, Appendix A, Section 2(c)(2)(iii) or in accordance with the instructions of the Call Report (12 CFR Part 3, Appendix A(c)(2)(ii)(A)&(B)).

  - The fair market value of each intangible asset included in Tier 1 capital is determined at least quarterly; the market value includes adjustments for any significant changes in original valuation assumptions including changes in prepayment estimates; and, in determining the current fair market value of the intangible asset, the bank applies an appropriate market discount rate to the expected net cash flows of the intangible asset (12 CFR Part 3, Appendix A(c)(2)(iii)).

- Any intangible assets other than mortgage servicing assets and purchased credit card relationships are deducted from the Tier 1 portion of the capital base before calculating the Tier 2 portion (12 CFR Part 3, Appendix A, Section 2(c)(1)(ii)).

For Tier 2 Capital requirements determine that:

- Tier 2 capital is no more than 100 percent of the bank's Tier 1 capital (12 CFR 3.6(a), Appendix A, Section 4(b)(3), and Table 4).

- Any preferred stock issues in which the dividend is reset periodically, based upon current market conditions and the bank's current credit rating, are assigned to Tier 2 capital (12 CFR Part 3, Appendix A, Section 2(a)(2)).

- The amount of the Allowance for Loan and Lease Losses in Tier 2 capital is limited to 1.25 percent of risk-weighted assets (12 CFR Part 3, Appendix A, Section 2(b)(1)).

- The bank's cumulative perpetual preferred stock, long-term preferred stock, convertible preferred stock, and any related surplus are included in the bank's Tier 2 capital (12 CFR Part 3, Appendix A, Section 2(b)(2)).

- The amount of any long-term preferred stock that is eligible as Tier 2 capital is reduced by 20 percent of the original amount of the instrument (net of redemptions) at the beginning of each of the last five years of the life of the instrument (12 CFR Part 3, Appendix A, Section 2(b)(2)).

- Any hybrid capital instruments included in the bank's Tier 2 capital meets the requirements of 12 CFR Part 3, Appendix A, Section 2(b)(3).

- Any term subordinated debt instruments, and intermediate-term preferred stock and related surplus are included in Tier 2 capital, but only to a maximum of 50 percent of Tier 1 capital (12 CFR Part 3, Appendix A, Section 2(b)(4)).

- Any term subordinated debt meets the requirements of 12 CFR 3.100(f)(1).

For Tier 3 Capital requirements determine:

- That national banks with significant exposure to market risk, comply 12 CFR Part 3, Appendix B (Risk-Based Capital Guidelines; Market Risk Adjustment).

For other requirements determine that:

- If noncompliance with the minimum capital ratio requirements of 12 CFR 3.7 exists, the bank has submitted to the OCC a plan describing the means and time schedule by which it will achieve the minimum ratios within 60 days of such noncompliance.

- Any asset deducted from a bank's capital in computing the capital base (numerator) of the risk-based capital ratio is also deducted from the bank's risk-weighted assets (denominator).

- Assets representing indirect holdings of a pool of assets, such as mutual funds, are assigned to the appropriate risk category. (12 CFR Part 3, Section 3).

- On-balance sheet assets have the appropriate risk- weighting (12 CFR Part 3,

Appendix A, Section 3(a)).

- Off-balance sheet activities have the appropriate conversion factor and risk-weighting (12 CFR Part 3, Appendix A, Section 3(b)).

- Capital requirements on transfers of small business obligations meet the criteria outlined in 12 CFR Part 3, Appendix A, Section 3(c).

2.   If a change in the outstanding voting stock resulted in a change in control of the bank as defined by 12 U.S.C. 1817(j), consider:

- Whether shareholders received prior notice and did not disapprove of the change in control.  (Prior notice requirements are contained in 12 CFR 5.50.)

- Whether the change was effected according to the specified terms.

- Whether any change in the chief executive officer or a director that occurred in the 12-month period following the change in control was reported to the OCC.

- Whether any appropriate notices were filed with the OCC.

3.   If applicable, review dividends since previous examination.  Consider:

- That transfers to surplus from undivided profits were correctly made until surplus equaled common capital before another dividend was declared and that the statutory requirements of 12 U.S.C. 60 have been met.

- That all preferred stock dividend requirements were met before any dividends were paid to common shareholders (*See* 12 U.S.C. 51b(b)).

- That no dividends have been paid that constitute a violation of law or regulation (*See* 12 U.S.C. 56 and 60).

4.   Determine the bank's compliance with transfer agent activity requirements.

For a bank that acts as transfer agent for its own securities and that has more than 500 shareholders and $1 million or more in assets at year-end:

- Determine that it has registered its stock with the OCC's Securities and Corporate Practices division as required by Section 12(g) of the Securities Exchange Act of 1934.

---

For a bank subject to the Securities Exchange Act of 1934 as amended and acting as transfer agent for its own stock:

- Test compliance with 12 CFR 9.20 by determining that:

  - Form TA-1 has been filed with the OCC declaring the bank a registered transfer agent.

  - Amendments have been filed within 60 days of any changes in the information on Form TA-1.

For a bank subject to the Securities Exchange Act of 1934 and acting as transfer agent for its own securities:

- Test compliance by reviewing the securities transfer and registrar procedures to determine that:

  - If the bank receives more than 500 items for transfer during any six consecutive month period, at least 90 percent of the routine items received during any given month are transferred within 3 business days (*See* Section 240.17Ad-2(a)).

  - If the bank receives more than 500 items for processing as registrar during any six consecutive month period, at least 90 percent of the routine items received during any given month are processed within one business day (*See* Section 240.17 Ad2(b)).

  - If the bank failed to meet those time requirements, a notice stating the reason for the failure, the number of unprocessed items and planned remedial action was filed with the OCC and the SEC within 10 days of the end of the month (*See* Section 240.17 Ad2(c)).

  - If the bank received less than 500 items for transfer and processing as registrar over any six consecutive month period, the bank has prepared and maintained a notice certifying that the transfer agent is qualified to be exempt from Section 240.17 Ad-4(b)(1).

  - All directors, officers, and employees involved in or with access to transfer agent activities have been fingerprinted (*See* Section 240.17 f-2(a)).

  - The bank maintains appropriate records in an accessible area for at least 3 years after the individual leaves the employment of the bank (*See* Section 240.17 f-2(d)).

# Quality of Risk Management

**Conclusion:** The quality of risk management is (strong, satisfactory, weak).

## Policy

**Conclusion:** The Board (has/does not have) adequate policies and practices for ensuring that capital and dividends are appropriate for the risk profile of the institution.

**Objective:** Assess the Board's policies regarding the adequacy of capital and dividends.

1.  Determine whether the board of directors, consistent with it duties and responsibilities, have adopted formal or informal capital and dividend policies. Consider:

    *   Whether policy requires a separation of duties between preparation of call reports (Schedule RC-R) and audits of the process.

    *   Whether policy addresses the size of the institution and the nature of its activities to ensure an adequate level of capital is maintained as well as an appropriate level of dividends.

    *   Whether management approval is required of the risk weighting of unusual assets.

    *   Whether the signing of blank stock certificates is prohibited.

2.  Determine that the bank periodically reviews its policies to ensure it reflects any changes in laws, rules, or regulations.

3.  Determine that bank management clearly and effectively communicates its policies governing capital and dividends to appropriate bank employees.

## Processes

**Conclusion:** The bank (has/does not have) effective processes for controlling risks to capital given the bank's scope of operations and risk profile.

**Objective:** To evaluate management processes for controlling risks to capital.

1.    Determine how the bank evaluates the adequacy of its capital to support present and planned activities.

2.    Determine how decisions are made on the specific risk-weighting of unusual assets.

3.    Determine if clear lines of authority and responsibility for monitoring adherence to policies, procedures, and limits been established by the Board and senior management.  Consider:

      • Have limits been defined and communicated to management?
      • Has a measurement system that captures and quantifies risk been established?
      • Do the planning, budgeting, and new product areas incorporate capital considerations?

4.    As appropriate, review working papers the bank uses to calculate its risk-based capital position and dividends to determine if decisions are supported.

5.    Determine the accuracy of capital changes since the previous examination. Consider:

      • Reconciling the proceeds of capital stock and notes sold to investment bankers' statements, prospectuses, option agreements, etc., and trace credit to the general ledger.

      • Checking disbursements (payments to underwriters, etc.) made in connection with the stock sale or notes issued to contracts, official approvals, or invoices.

      • Determining that proceeds received for notes attributable to conversion features or warrants to purchase capital stock are properly accounted for.

      • Reviewing conversion and redemption transactions for compliance with contractual agreements.

6.    Determine the accuracy of dividends issued since the last examination. Consider:

      • Checking the computation of dividends paid by multiplying the number of shares outstanding at each dividend date by the appropriate per share amounts approved by the board of directors.

      • Reviewing and documenting, by memorandum, the flow of dividends from authorization to payment, and determine that the liability added immediately after declaration of any dividend is equal in amount to the cash dividend declared.

- Reviewing the status of any cumulative preferred dividends in arrears.

- Reviewing and determining the propriety of the handling of unclaimed dividend checks.

7.   Review the bank's process for making entries to undivided profits and determine if entries are appropriate.  Consider:

- Closing of income and expense.
- Payment of dividends.
- Increases or decreases due to consolidations or mergers.
- Extraordinary items not normally included in the income and expense account (such items are expected to be rare).
- Authorized transfers to or from surplus and contingency reserve account.

8.   Determine if adequate controls and processes exist for stock and dividend records.

- Has the board of directors passed a resolution designating those officers who are authorized to:
    - Sign stock certificates?
    - Maintain custody of unissued stock certificates?
    - Sign dividend checks?
    - Maintain stock journals and records?

- Are capital transactions independently verified before stock certificates are issued?

- Are persons responsible for the handling of stock certificates and debentures independent from those responsible for recording those transactions?

- Does the bank maintain a stock certificate book with certificates serially numbered by the printer?

- Is the stock certificate book maintained under dual control?

- Does the bank maintain a shareholders' ledger that reflects the total number of shares owned by each stockholder?

- Does the bank maintain a stock transfer journal disclosing names, dates, and amounts of transactions?

- Are surrendered stock certificates canceled?

- Are unused dividend checks under dual control?

- Does the bank's control process require separation of duties regarding custody, authorization, preparation, signing, and distribution of dividend checks?

- Are dividend checks reconciled in detail before mailing?

- Is control maintained over the use of serially numbered dividend checks to ensure they are issued sequentially?

If the bank acts as its own transfer agent:

- Are outstanding stock and notes verified by reference to open stubs in the stock and note certificate book?

- Are inventories of unissued notes or debentures maintained under dual control?

- Are inventories counted periodically by someone other than the person(s) responsible for their custody?

- Are all unissued stock and note certificates accounted for properly?

- Are misprinted and mutilated certificates canceled and accounted for properly?

- When transfers are made:

  - Are notes and debentures surrendered and promptly canceled?

  - Are surrendered notes or debentures inspected to determine that proper assignment has been made and that the new notes or debentures agree in amount?

If the bank has an outside transfer agent and/or registrar consider:

- Requesting confirmation from the transfer agent of total shares and notes issued and unbilled fees.

- Requesting confirmation from the registrar of the total shares and notes authorized, the total shares and notes issued, and unbilled fees.

- Checking information confirmed by the transfer agent and registrar.

## Personnel

**Conclusion:** The board, management, and effected personnel (do/do not) possess the skills and knowledge required to manage and perform duties related to capital and dividends.

**Objective:** Given the size and complexity of the bank, determine if the board and management possess the knowledge required or engage competent personnel to address capital and dividend issues.

1. Determine significant current and previous work experience of the board, management and other capital and dividends personnel. Consider:

    - Specialized experience in public and private stock offerings.
    - Experience in transfer agent duties.
    - Strategic planning experience.
    - Legal and accounting experience.
    - Risk management experience.

2. If external resources are used for capital and dividend issues, consider:

    - Range of specialized experience in public and private stock offerings.
    - Experience in transfer agent activities.
    - Strategic planning experience.
    - Legal and accounting experience.

3. Determine how expertise was obtained for both bank personnel and external resources. Consider:

    - Professional designations.
    - Education.
    - Work experience.

4. Assess technical knowledge and ability to manage capital and dividends.

Consider determination of the quantity of risk.

# Controls

Conclusion: Management (has/has not) established effective control systems.

Objective: To determine if the bank's control systems are effective, given the level of risk and sophistication of banking activities.

1.  Determine if the internal or external audit and/or compliance officer review for compliance with laws, rulings, regulations, and internal policies and procedures for capital and dividends.  Consider:

    *   That independent validation is required of the assignment of the appropriate risk-weighting for on and off-balance sheet transactions.

    *   Their function is adequate in terms of independence, scope, coverage, and frequency of review.

    *   They review risk-based capital for accuracy and compliance with laws, rulings, and regulations and any other capital or dividend statute or regulation.

    *   They review dividend payments for compliance with 12 U.S.C. 51, 56, 59, 60 and 12 CFR 5.6.

    *   They review change of control in bank stock for compliance with 12 U.S.C. 1817(j) and 12 CFR 5.50.

    *   They report results of reviews of capital and dividend issues to the board of directors or committee.

2.  Determine if bank management takes timely corrective action to address capital deficiencies noted by the audit and/or compliance functions.  Consider:

    *   Are recommendations for corrective action monitored to ensure timely follow-up?

    *   Are personnel held accountable for implementing corrective measures in timely fashion?

3.  Using the work performed by the auditors or compliance officer, select a sample of bank products, including off-balance sheet products, and verify the accuracy and completeness of their findings relative to compliance with risk-based capital

rules. If no audit or compliance function exists, determine if the bank's process is sufficient to ensure the integrity of risk-based capital calculations and compliance with applicable laws, rulings, and regulations.

# Conclusion Procedures

For a bank with a Capital component rating of 1 or 2, use the following procedures:

1. Determine the Capital Component Rating using the rating elements provided in OCC 97-1.

2. Provide EIC with brief conclusion.

3. Determine the impact on the aggregate and direction of risk assessments for any applicable risks identified by performing the above procedures. Examiners should refer to guidance provided under the OCC's large and community bank risk assessment programs. Consider:

   - Risk Categories: Compliance, Credit, Foreign Currency Translation, Interest Rate, Liquidity, Price, Reputation, Strategic, Transaction
   - Risk Conclusions: High, Moderate, or Low
   - Risk Direction: Increasing, Stable, or Decreasing

4. Determine in consultation with EIC, if the risks identified are significant enough to merit bringing them to the board's attention in the report of examination. If so, prepare items for inclusion under the heading Matters Requiring Board Attention (MRBA).

   - MRBA should cover practices that:
     - Deviate from sound fundamental principles and are likely to result in financial deterioration if not addressed.
     - Result in substantive noncompliance with laws.

   - MRBA should discuss:
     - Causative factors contributing to the problem.
     - Consequences of inaction.
     - Management's commitment for corrective action.
     - The time frame and person(s) responsible for corrective action.

5. Discuss findings with management including conclusions regarding applicable risks.

6. As appropriate, prepare a Capital comment for inclusion in the report of examination.

7. Prepare a memorandum or update the work program with any information that will

facilitate future examinations.

8.  Update the OCC's electronic information system and any applicable report of examination schedules or tables.

9.  Organize and reference working papers in accordance with OCC guidance.

For a bank with a Capital component rating of 3 or worse, use the following procedures:

1.  Determine the Capital Component Rating using rating elements described in OCC 97-1.

2.  Provide a detailed conclusion comment to the EIC.

3.  Determine the impact on the aggregate and direction of risk assessments for any applicable risks identified by performing the above procedures. Examiners should refer to guidance provided under the OCC's large and community bank risk assessment programs.  Consider:

    - Risk Categories:        Compliance, Credit, Foreign Currency Translation, Interest Rate, Liquidity, Price, Reputation, Strategic, Transaction
    - Risk Conclusions: High, Moderate, or Low
    - Risk Direction:        Increasing, Stable, or Decreasing

4.  Determine in consultation with EIC, which of the risks identified are significant enough to merit bringing them to the board's attention in the report of examination. If so, prepare items for inclusion under the heading Matters Requiring Board Attention.  Consider:

    - MRBA should cover practices that:
        - Deviate from sound fundamental principles and are likely to result in financial deterioration if not addressed.
        - Result in substantive noncompliance with laws.

    - MRBA should discuss:
        - Causative factors contributing to the problem.
        - Consequences of inaction.
        - Management's commitment for corrective action.
        - The time frame and person(s) responsible for corrective action.

5.  Discuss findings with management including conclusions regarding applicable

risks.

6.      Develop, in consultation with the EIC, a strategy to address the bank's weaknesses and discuss the strategy with the appropriate supervisory office or manager.

7.      Prepare a Capital comment for inclusion in the report of examination.

8.      Prepare a memorandum or update the work program with any information that will facilitate future examinations.

9.      Update the OCC's electronic information system and any applicable report of examination schedules or tables.

10.     Organize and reference working papers in accordance with OCC guidance.